Learning the Pacific Way

A Guide for All Ages

Janet M. DeVries

Friendship Press • New York

BV
3670
.D41
1982

ISBN: 0-377-00119-8

Copyright © 1982 by Friendship Press, Inc.

Editorial Offices: 475 Riverside Drive, New York, NY 10115
Distribution Offices: P.O. Box 37844, Cincinnati, OH 45237

Printed in the United States of America

CONTENTS

1. Introduction 5
2. The Pacific Islands: An Overview 11
3. Study Sessions 19
   Session 1. Learning About the Pacific Islands
       and Their People 19
   Session 2. Independence: People and Nations 23
   Session 3. People of the Pacific Islands
       Speak About Their History and Culture 26
   Session 4. Stewardship: A Biblical and
       Cultural Issue 32
   Session 5. The Vision: A Nuclear-Free Pacific 34
   Session 6. Participants in a Global Community:
       Personal Involvement 40
4. Children Experience the Pacific Islands 45
   Session 1 52
   Session 2 54
   Session 3 55
   Session 4 57
   Session 5 59
5. Additional Resources 61

1. Introduction

tran•si•tion /n/ the passage from one place, state, stage of development to another; a change; also, the period, place, passage in which such a change is effected.

The people of the Pacific islands are in transition. They are moving from one place to another, sometimes from one culture to another; they are changing, and not always with the satisfaction of believing that change is "better."

Politically, probably no other area of the world has seen so many countries become independent in such a short period of time. Independence both causes and is caused by change and transition.

In any "coming of age," whether for a person or a people, transition periods are times for rejoicing and times for weeping. Such is the case with the Pacific islands. There are great natural and human resources in the Pacific islands; there is also potential for exploitation. The Pacific Ocean is vast; its vastness tempts some to use those waters for nuclear testing. War and destruction are part of recent history in the Pacific islands; there is also a desire to live interdependently with the land in an area influenced by different attitudes from Asia and the West.

Transitions: the Pacific islands are in transition to a new place in the global community — politically, socially and religiously. It is appropriate for us to study the Pacific islands; it is essential for us to be informed about the issues, attitudes and feelings of the Pacific island people.

Using This Guide

This guide is based on a premise about learning—that people of all ages learn most effectively when given opportunities to interact with one another, to discover resources for themselves and participate in different kinds of activities, and to test and put to use newfound information.

To help groups engage in a meaningful learning process, this guide contains several different kinds of information. Included in this introductory section is an explanation of the learning resource center, including detailed descriptions of the Friendship Press materials prepared especially for this study. Chapter 2 includes a section of factual background on four areas of the Pacific.

Detailed session plans for use with adult and youth groups follow. A special section, "Children Experience the Pacific Islands," provides detailed guidance and activity suggestions for teachers of early and late elementary children, and includes ideas for an intergenerational celebration.

Finally, a bibliography of additional resources guides those who wish to pursue specific topics in greater depth.

To grow to adulthood in the Pacific is to learn through individual experiences, family and extended family relationships. What is learned is a way of life, a set of values, a reverence for the created world, interdependence with that world and a relationship with its creator God. These are valuable lessons for children, youth and adults in any culture.

The Purpose and Development of the Learning Resource Center

Development of a learning resource center will help groups to make most effective use of this study guide. A *learning resource center* is a special area in a classroom, church library or other convenient location where material related to issues in the Pacific islands can be assembled and displayed. Both print and nonprint materials may be included.

A learning resource center can be as simple or as elaborate as you care to make it. If you have an area where you can leave the materials for the duration of the study, this is ideal. If you must dismantle the center between sessions, however, store the contents in large boxes or in a storage area. Do not be discouraged by physical limitations; use your creativity!

The learning resource center is designed to focus attention on the following areas:
- study and research on the Pacific islands;
- pressing social issues of the region;
- understanding the people of the Pacific islands — their hopes, plans, attitudes, culture.

Draw the attention of persons in the congregation and church community to the learning resource center through publicity in the newsletter, posters or announcements in the Sunday bulletin. If members of your congregation have not used learning resource centers before, your effective use of one during this study may lead to development of centers for other issues, concerns or programs in the church's life.

Resources For This Study

At the core of the learning center will be the Friendship Press resources prepared especially for this study. The session plans in this study guide are based on these materials, and you will want to have multiple copies of the basic book for the members of your group. Friendship Press resources may be secured from the store or agency from which you usually purchase religious resources, or may be ordered in quantity from: Friendship Press Distribution Office, P.O. Box 37844, Cincinnati, Ohio 45237.

- *Pacific People Sing Out Strong,* edited by William L. Coop. $4.95. The basic text for the study; introduces Pacific people and their views on current challenges and issues through prose, poetry and photos.
- *Follow the Sun...to Tahiti, to Western Samoa, to Fiji, to Melanesia, to Micronesia,* by Gweneth Deverell. $3.95. Five story papers introduce early elementary children to Pacific families through stories, pictures and activity ideas.
- *Come to My Place: Meet My Island Family,* Stories from the Pacific compiled by Esiteri Kamikamica. $4.95. Stories and facts about the Pacific for older elementary children.
- *Map 'n' Facts: Pacific Islands,* 35" × 23", $3.50. A geographical perspective on the Pacific, including enlargements of six island groups and up-to-date "facts" section.
- *People of the Silver Sea,* Bill Matthews. Color filmstrip with cassette, script/guidance booklet. $18.95. Introduces viewers to Micronesia, Melanesia and Polynesia; includes separate script and soundtrack for use with children.

- *To Live Among the Stars: Christian Origins in Oceania,* by John Garrett. Cloth $17.95; paper $12.95. The story of Catholic and Protestant expansion in the Pacific; published jointly by the University of the South Pacific, Fiji and the World Council of Churches' Programme on Theological Education, Geneva. For the serious student and for leaders' background.

Books and Other Printed Material

If your church library includes material related to the Pacific islands, use it as part of the book collection for the learning resource center. Contact your local public library or county library service for additional books to borrow for the study. See "Additional Resources," chapter 5 of this guide, for suggestions.

A brief annotated bibliography describing each of the available books should be developed to encourage readers.

You may find that various kinds of descriptive brochures, pamphlets and periodicals dealing with the Pacific islands are more readily available than books. At transitional times in the Pacific, periodicals most likely will feature updates on such issues as shifts in leadership in the trust territories of Micronesia. One excellent source of information is through the local/regional United Nations Association chapter, or through the resource offices in New York City.

An excellent source of descriptive information about the Pacific, as well as other parts of the world, is *National Geographic* magazine. This may be one of the best sources for pictures and brief descriptions of cultural life. Check back issues and display relevant ones in your learning center.

Another source of pictorial material would be travel agencies. If you use this source, however, be aware that tourists do not share the perspective of the Pacific peoples themselves and may, in fact, represent exploitation of the region. A study of the impact of tourism would be one possibility for a group project.

Map Displays

The use of a map during the study is essential. *Map 'n' Facts: Pacific Islands* has been prepared especially for this course. Use it to develop the following displays.

Migration. Island people have migrated through the years from one section of the Pacific to another. Using colored paper strips or yarn, show the movement of various groups. Add to the factual information on the map by providing a supplementary folder for topical information, which may be added throughout the course. Invite people to use this resource freely. Various sources will provide different ideas about how people moved and their reasons for doing so.

Natural Resources. Some Pacific islands are volcanic and provide especially fertile ground for growing various crops. One issue in the Pacific has to do with economic rights of the nations to use their resources and/or the money resulting from development of their resources. Use paper symbols, different colored pins or some such method to identify on the map the different natural resources in the Pacific. As you find printed material about each of the countries' resources, put that in the supplementary folder you have provided to accompany the map.

Political Independence. Trace the development of independent nations. In addition, you might want to use a code to identify the former colonial powers and the distribution of their land occupation in the Pacific islands. You might also want to identify the particular forms of government each of the countries has selected and how those correspond to former colonial governments.

Interest Areas
Projects that may be developed from materials in the learning resource center are limited only by your imagination. Here are a few ideas.

Audiovisuals. If possible, provide a quiet area for individual or small group viewing of audiovisual materials. *People of the Silver Sea* has been prepared especially for this study, and comes with a cassette that includes some indigenous music. A separate script and soundtrack for use with children is also included.

If anyone in your community has traveled to the Pacific, you might be able to obtain slides from the region and prepare a slide show of your own. Be sure to choose slides carefully so that they will communicate to as many people as possible, and not simply to those who know their owner.

Art and Music. Information about the many art forms and handicrafts that are such an important part of the various cultures of the Pacific is included in the study materials. Check "Additional Resources" for details and how-to-do-it guidelines. Search for examples of the arts and crafts of the Pacific. Explore their importance to the culture and economy.

Learn the songs included in *Pacific People Sing Out Strong* and the children's materials, *Follow the Sun* and *Come to My Place: Meet My Island Family.*

This area of exploration may well provide some good opportunities for intergenerational sharing.

Foods. In chapter 4, the children's section of this guide, are suggestions for an intergenerational celebration. One aspect of this is sharing foods typical of the Pacific region. If some members of the group can locate recipes, these might be tested. A group might plan and prepare a menu for a closing celebration. Again, persons of all ages could work together on projects related to foods.

Worship. Plan a worship experience or experiences based on what you discover about Pacific forms and practices. Material in the Friendship Press resources will get you started.

2. The Pacific Islands: An Overview

Covering almost one-third of the earth's surface, the Pacific Ocean is home for approximately 21 million people. New Zealand and Australia account for almost 16 million of these, leaving 5 million people scattered across a large number of smaller island nations.

The Pacific islands are often divided into island groups: *Micronesia* is in the northwest and includes the Marianas, Caroline Islands, Marshall Islands, Tuvalu and Kiribati; *Melanesia* includes Papua New Guinea, Fiji, the Solomon Islands, Vanuatu (formerly New Hebrides) and New Caledonia; and *Polynesia,* east and northeast, includes Hawaii, Western Samoa, American Samoa, Tonga, Tahiti, the Marquesas and the Cook Islands. *Map 'n' Facts: Pacific Islands* provides more information about the geography of the Pacific.

Migration to the Pacific islands is thought to have been from Asia, despite the popularized theory of Thor Heyerdahl that the people are "American" in their cultural patterns. It is thought that, as early as 6000 B.C., people who survive today as aborigines in Australia and as mountain people in Papua New Guinea settled in these locations as others traveled on to other places in Melanesia. From their dark brown skin came the name *Melanesia,* meaning "islands of dark-skinned people." Several thousand years later, it is thought, other people traveled across the ocean and settled in the Polynesian islands. These lighter-skinned people formed *Polynesia,* or "many islands." Later, a small migration settled the islands now known as *Micronesia,* or "tiny islands."

Although these main groups are in many ways similar to one another, over a period of time significant cultural and language patterns have also evolved within each group. One consequence of the separation of communities by water and by miles is the variety of languages. Although a form of English is understood by many Pacific Islanders, the number of indigenous languages reflects the richness and diversity of these particular cultures. In Papua New Guinea, for example, the number of languages has reached about 700, although an English "pidgin" is used widely.

Although more will be said about the lifestyles and attitudes of the people, it should be noted that the people of the Pacific islands have learned to interact with the land and sea in such a way that these elements yield what the people need for physical survival. North Americans have much to learn from the island way of life. In Rabaul, Papua New Guinea, for example, malnutrition is less of a problem than it is in the capital city of Port Moresby. In Rabaul, the people survive comfortably on fruits and vegetables and pork, which are a natural part of their village environment. But when individuals leave such an environment and move to a city like Port Moresby, providing necessities means getting a job with a sufficient wage to pay for rent and food. This is only one example of the transition that Pacific Islanders are experiencing as they discover the positive and negative features of development.

Brief Sketches of Four Countries

Vanuatu

In 1980, the New Hebrides became the independent nation of Vanuatu, ending a period of colonial rule by France and Great Britain that began in 1906. In his independence address to the nation, Prime Minister Father Walter Lini made the following comments:

> ...we shall need guidance not only from God but from our own custom and traditional values. We are moving into a period of rapid change rather like a canoe entering a patch of rough water: God and custom must be the sail and the steering-paddle of our canoe. It will be the responsibility of successive parliaments and governments as well as the chiefs to preserve our custom but not to preserve it blindly and without reference to change. For custom has always changed with people's ideas and it must continue to do so.
> ...The future of Vanuatu is bright, and it is important that we should be allowed to develop in the Melanesian way on our own. As a nation we put our colonial past behind us and step confidently into a new future. We will go beyond pandemonium to the independence of a free Pacific Islands territory, and look forward to taking our place among the nations of the world.*

---

*Walter Lini, *Beyond Pandemonium* (Wellington, N.Z.: Asia Pacific Books, 1980), pp. 62-63.

The words of Father Walter Lini are indicative of the spirit of independence among the Pacific island nations. His ideas are set forth in more detail in two selections in the basic study book for this emphasis, *Pacific People Sing Out Strong*. The challenge is to preserve the best of the cultural norms and values, while recognizing development as a tool for participation in an interdependent global community. It is significant that Father Lini's election as prime minister confirmed his long-term efforts for independence. Others in the new government of Vanuatu, such as President Ati George Sokomanu, likewise represent a long-term commitment.

The history of Vanuatu dates back to 1300 B.C., the probable date when the island was first inhabited. First contact with the Western world came in 1606, when a Spanish explorer visited. The name New Hebrides (recalling islands off Scotland's west coast) was given to the islands by Captain James Cook in 1774. As with other Pacific islands, the first visitors were explorers, traders and missionaries. French and British settlers grew in number until joint supervision by the two European nations was agreed upon in 1888. The United States built two large military bases at Vila and Santo during World War II, so the presence of non-Melanesian powers has been a predominant experience. Political organizations began appearing in the 1960s, working with the United Nations to secure independence. France and Britain were for many years reluctant to see independence. In recent years, however, the British recognized its inevitability and pressured the French, who remained reluctant, to work toward the planned independence that was achieved in 1980. The new government has sought to work closely with the former colonial powers, knowing that transitions take time. Both Britain and France have committed substantial monies for the development of Vanuatu, although France has been slow to fulfill its commitment.

The nation itself consists of about 80 islands, covering an area of 11,800 square kilometers, with 12 islands being the predominant ones. The islands are on a volcanic crest, and five volcanoes are still somewhat active. The volcanic deposits result in a mountainous terrain.

The people of Vanuatu are predominantly Melanesian and speak a variety of languages. Some people in the outer islands consider themselves Polynesians. The islands are sparsely populated, with a total population of about 113,000. Many villages are inland in the mountains, although over half of the people live close to the sea.

Most of the population is engaged in some form of agriculture, growing such crops as yams, taro, manioc and breadfruit. Coffee, cocoa and copra (dried coconut meat, which yields coconut oil) are also produced, and cattle are raised on some islands. Copra exports provide the largest income for the country, with beef also being a significant export. One of the changes independence has brought is the shift from European-owned farms to indigenous ownership and development.

Since independence, Vanuatu has experienced some internal political difficulty, particularly with residents of the island of Espiritu Santo. For additional information, see Prime Minister Walter Lini's articles, "Vanuatu Enters the United Nations" and "True Independence in the Pacific Islands" in *Pacific People Sing Out Strong*.

Fiji

On October 10, 1970, Fiji became an independent dominion of the British Commonwealth. Since that time, Fiji has been one of the most stable countries in the Pacific.

Probably one of the earliest island groups to be settled, Fiji first experienced European presence via the Dutch in 1643. However, indications are that Fiji was settled as early as 3000 B.C. The islands were annexed by Great Britain in 1874 after some turmoil from surrounding islands, and particularly from the Tongan chief, Ma'afu.

Fiji's first colonial governor agreed to bring indentured workers from India to work in the sugar fields. Most Indians decided to stay in Fiji, and today over half of the population is Indian. As the country sought independence, representation agreements for Fijians, Indians and Europeans were worked out so that all groups are represented in a House of Representatives and a Senate.

Suva, the capital, is one of the more developed cities in the Pacific. A number of international agencies have established their South Pacific headquarters there. The offices of the Pacific Conference of Churches are in Suva, directly across from the government buildings.

Although the majority of Fiji's population resides on the two largest islands of Viti Levu and Vanua Levu, the country itself consists of more than 300 islands, of which 105 are populated. Both of the main islands have several rivers. With few exceptions, the islands of Fiji were formed through volcanic action. The climate is generally quite wet with some parts of the islands receiving more rainfall than others.

Fiji is the home of the University of the South Pacific and the Pacific Theological College. The Fiji School of Medicine trains medical personnel for a number of the Pacific islands. Some schools are run by the government; others are operated by churches or local community committees.

Fiji's primary export is sugar. Coconut oil, copra, timber, gold, bananas, and green ginger are also exported. Some manganese mining is also done in the western section of Viti Levu.

In part because of its central location in the Pacific, and probably also because of its connection with the British Commonwealth, Fiji hosts major sea and air traffic in the Pacific islands. The airport at Nadi is able to accommodate large planes, connecting Fiji with North America, east Asia and the rest of the world.

Papua New Guinea

Papua New Guinea is a member of the British Commonwealth, having become independent in 1975. The government follows a parliamentary system with an elected national legislative assembly, prime minister and cabinet, and an appointed governor-general who is head of state. Provincial government developed after independence with a premier as head of each province.

The island of New Guinea may have been inhabited as early as 30,000 years ago through migrations from Asia. The first European to arrive was Jorge de Meneses in 1526 who called the island *dos Papuas,* using the Malay word meaning "frizzy-haired." The name of New Guinea was given to the island by a Spaniard who was reminded by the people of the inhabitants of the Guinea coast of Africa. Through the centuries, the land was divided up and annexed by different countries. In 1828, the western half of the main island (now Irian Jaya) was annexed by the Dutch.

In 1884, the Germans claimed the northern half and the British claimed the southern half and its islands, which later became known as British New Guinea. The Germans operated from Rabaul (on the island of New Britain) and incorporated several of the Micronesian island groups in 1899. By 1906, British New Guinea had become a possession of Australia and was renamed Papua.

Wars fought in other parts of the world affected the governing of the Papua and New Guinea areas. After World War I, Australia became responsible for land previously governed by the Germans. The islands were administered from Rabaul and Port Moresby (now the capital) until the Japanese invaded in 1941. After World War II, Australia determined to administer both areas jointly. It was not until 1971 that the name of the country was changed from the territory of Papua and New Guinea to Papua New Guinea. Independence and change in government has evolved over a period of several years since then.

As was true with many countries that are now independent in the Pacific islands, different colonial powers developed a variety of industries to satisfy economic interests. While some of these have left a base for national economic structure, others have been exploitive.

Leadership in Papua New Guinea represents a variety of people, cultures and languages. The island of New Guinea (part of the country) is the second largest island in the world. Only Greenland is larger. (Australia is deemed to be a continent rather than an island.) Much of Papua New Guinea, including the island of New Guinea, is mountainous as a result of volcanic activity. Swampy areas lie between the central mountain ranges and the coast. In the interior are a series of valleys and some jungle. Some of the people in the interior did not come in contact with Westerners until about forty years ago. Throughout the islands of Papua New Guinea, over 700 languages are spoken. Many people understand English, but pidgin is the most common language used by the people.

The country itself encompasses great distances, so air transportation is important. Papua New Guinea has its own airline, which provides interisland travel on a regular basis. The land is too rugged to be traversed by automobile, and sea travel is not used consistently. The capital city, Port Moresby, on the surface appears quite westernized. However, the contrast between the subsistence living by simple farming in rural areas and the poverty of the city is striking.

Education is provided by an increasing number of secondary schools, the University of Papua New Guinea and institutions for agriculture, forestry and technical work. Land ownership is usually acquired by birth into landholding groups. Farming is usually subsistence level and open-air markets feature sweet potato, taro, coconuts, a variety of bananas, sugarcane, peanuts and tobacco. Copra and coconut products top the list of exports, with rubber, cocoa beans, coffee beans and timber also represented. Mineral exploration is prevalent, and most important is the copper mining operation on the island of Bougainville.

It is interesting to note that the first Christian missionaries to these islands came from Fiji. Earlier mission work in Tonga (1822), Samoa (1828) and Fiji (1835) had led to the development of Christian communities there. In 1871, the Rev. George Brown, a

Methodist missionary in Samoa, suggested that the people of these three island groupings should send missionaries to the people of New Guinea. Students from Tonga, Samoa and Fiji went with Brown to become missionaries to New Guinea. Eventually, after a series of efforts by several churches, the United Church of Papua New Guinea and the Solomon Islands was formed as an indigenous church. From the beginning, national leadership was utilized far more readily than were European missionaries.

Micronesia

The history of Micronesia is a story of cultural and political domination. The hope that emerges is one of movement toward self-government. The year 1982 presumably marks the end of United Nations "trust territory" status, although it is clear that the United States expects to continue to exert major influence in the islands.

Micronesia, although it includes over 2,000 islands, is small in terms of population. Some 125,000 people live on the fewer than 100 inhabited islands. Culturally and historically, the differences they encompass are tremendous. When the islands became a United Nations Trust Territory, they were divided into seven districts for administrative purposes. These districts are Yap, Truk, Ponape, Kosrae, Palau, the Marshall Islands and the Mariana Islands. In those territories, nine major languages are spoken.

In 1975, the Mariana Islands voted to become a trust of the United States. The Marshall Islands and Palau have voted to become separate nations and the remaining districts have become the Federated States of Micronesia.

Since 1521, these islands have been governed in succession by Spain, Germany, Japan and the United States. The third of these turned over the territory at the end of World War II. Of the four, Japan has been the most successful in developing agriculture and the economic facets of the islands.

World War II marked a change in the Micronesian islands. Some of the most severe battles of the war were fought in these Pacific waters. The United States used the Marshalls for nuclear testing. It was here, for example, that the first atom and hydrogen bombs were exploded. Planes headed for Nagasaki and Hiroshima left from one of the Mariana islands — Tinian, just below Saipan on the *Map 'n' Facts*.

It is hardly surprising that following World War II, the United States was interested in maintaining a strong presence in this part of the Pacific. Micronesia became one of 11 Trust Territories of the

United Nations in 1947, and the United States was given authority to administer it. The purpose of the trust relationship was "To promote the political, economic, social and educational advancement of the inhabitants...and their progressive development toward self-government or independence as may be appropriate." The trust agreement also discouraged fragmentation of the territory, meaning that independence of separate island nations was not seen as desirable.

Ten of the 11 trust territories have already become independent. But as the agreement moves to an end, the territory has not become completely independent.

What is proposed is a Compact of Free Association. In shorthand, the agreement gives the countries decision-making powers for internal concerns, but gives the United States primary clout for foreign affairs. For example, the countries will be governed by the compact for at least 15 years, thus making it impossible for them to seek membership in the United Nations. The United States retains authority for security and defense concerns in each area, and thus can sustain its own interests. The Compact of Free Association defines this in greater detail.

Concern has been expressed by a number of parties that the United States may not have provided for adequate political, economic and social development. Although appropriations rose from approximately $6 million in 1960 to approximately $60 million in 1970, little effort was made to clarify whether the needs being met were indeed the concerns of the Micronesian people, or to determine the effect of such "aid" on centuries-old cultural patterns.

The transplanted public school system, which served United States families living on military bases (such as the Kwajalein Missile Range in the Marshall Islands) and others, generally overlooked the Micronesian culture and experience. As one would guess, a long-term result has been the alienation of young Micronesians from their own culture through education. In order to use their education they often find that they have to leave Micronesia rather than to turn their energies into the region. Increasing evidence of drug abuse, alcoholism and suicide appear to be directly related to this problem.

During the next 15 years, under the Compact of Free Association, the Micronesian people must somehow seek to develop new leadership that reflects the renewed appreciation for their culture and respect for their traditions.

3. Study Sessions

Session 1: Learning About the Pacific Islands and Their People

Objectives:
1. To become informed about the Pacific islands and their people.
2. To develop basic knowledge as a foundation for further study.

Relevant Study Materials:

Pacific People Sing Out Strong, William L. Coop, particularly the section "Pacific Nations Statistics"
Map 'n' Facts: Pacific Islands
People of the Silver Sea (filmstrip)

Before the sessions begin, leaders will need to set up the learning resource center, using ideas from chapter 1 of this guide. The group should be encouraged to add to it during the course of the study, but participants will need some basic sources of information in order to complete the survey that introduces the course.

In this as in all the sessions, group leaders will need to pick and choose and adapt ideas from this guide to fit their specific time schedule, to meet the needs of the study group and to conform to the physical limitations of the meeting space.

Information Survey

As participants gather, hand out the following questionnaire and ask them to complete it. This is not a test; it is a method of discovering the varieties of knowledge and attitudes we have about the Pacific islands and their people. It is intended as a learning stimulus to prompt further reflection and work in the resource center. Use the *Map 'n' Facts* and *Pacific People Sing Out Strong* as resources in completing some of the questions. Take about 20 minutes to do this.

1. Name three Pacific island countries that have become independent in the past ten years. (*Vanuatu, Papua New Guinea, Solomon Islands, Tuvalu, Kiribati*)
2. What are the predominant languages of the Pacific islands? (*English, French, many native languages*)
3. What Protestant denominations have done significant mission work in the Pacific islands? (*Methodists, Presbyterians*)
4. What religious organization, founded in 1966, brought Christians together in the Pacific islands? (*Pacific Conference of Churches*)
5. Name the political leader of at least one country in the Pacific islands. (*Prime Minister Father Walter Lini, Vanatu*)
6. After which explorer of the Pacific islands is one group of islands named? (*Captain James Cook*)
7. What are at least two reasons the Pacific island nations wish to become independent? (*to preserve native cultures; because of their feelings about nuclear proliferation; because of conflicts over European rule and influence*)
8. Name one country where World War II left major military damage. (*Papua New Guinea*)
9. Name one country in Polynesia, one in Melanesia and one in Micronesia. (*refer to Map 'n' Facts: Pacific Islands*)
10. What is the meaning of each of these words: polynesia, melanesia, micronesia? (*polynesia = many islands; melanesia = islands of dark-skinned people; micronesia = tiny islands*)
11. Name one kind of fruit grown in the Pacific islands that is not normally a part of the North American diet. (*mangoes, guava, breadfruit*)
12. Name the starchy root vegetable grown and eaten in the Pacific islands that is a basic food staple there. (*taro*)

13. Identify at least one major social or political issue of the Pacific islands. (*independence, nuclear proliferation*)
14. What country took in indentured servants from a group that now makes up half the population? From what country did these people come? (*Fiji, India*)
15. What is the name of a form of English spoken in some of the Melanesian islands? (*pidgin*)
16. What countries currently influence policy and aid in the Pacific Islands? In what ways? (*Australia, United States, Great Britain, Japan, New Zealand; tourism, foreign aid, corporate personnel*)
17. In what way has the United Nations been involved in the Pacific islands? (*establishing trust territories in Micronesia following World War II*)
18. Name three countries considering or having completed nuclear testing in the Pacific islands. (*United States, France, Japan*)
19. What attitudes about war and independence do you think people in the Pacific islands may have as a result of World War II? (*opinions will vary*)

When group members have answered as many questions as they can, ask them to find someone else in the group with whom to discuss their answers and to share information. Take about 15 minutes to do this.

Come back together as a group. Discuss, in plenary, the following questions:
1. Were you surprised by what you did or did not know about the Pacific islands and their people?
2. What insights did you have about the issues that might affect an area of the world where countries are becoming independent?
3. What didn't you know that you would like to find out? Do you know where to go to get this information?
4. Identify one or two things you want to learn during this course of study.
5. What attitudes of your own did you discover in completing the questionnaire? Do you have any images or attitudes of the Pacific islands and their people that might be expanded or focused differently?

On a piece of newsprint, list the things all participants want to learn during the course of this study of the Pacific islands. Leaders should design future activities with this list in mind. Participants should add relevant materials to the learning resource center. Be alert to specific interests. Build in time in each session for sharing new information or insights gathered since the last time together. Recognize that the varied skills and interests and experiences represented in your group are resources in and of themselves! Plan time for dialogue and conversation in each session.

Viewing a Filmstrip

The filmstrip *People of the Silver Sea* should be previewed in advance and should be in place for use at this time. An introduction of the focus of the filmstrip and points to watch for should be given prior to viewing by the group. Ask people to watch for the following things as they view the filmstrip:

1. information about one of the Pacific island countries formerly unknown to them;
2. the importance of the sea and the land to Pacific island people;
3. at least three issues of *transition* among the Pacific island nations and people;
4. ways in which United States influence might be both advantageous and hazardous;
5. the role and function of the Christian church and issues it has identified for its work.

After viewing the filmstrip, ask people to share their responses to the above topics in small groups of not more than five persons. After 10 to 15 minutes, ask one person from each group to report about the responses. Were any questions from the first part of the session answered by the filmstrip? What method, if any, does the group wish to take to gather answers to questions in the questionnaire?

Reflection Time

This closing time is one of summary and thoughtfulness about what has happened during this first study session. Leaders should be prepared to reflect sensitively to the group on the ways in which the people interacted and the issues that have been addressed, and to set the focus for reading and reflection for the next meeting. Leaders might also raise the question of implications for the North American church in the issues of importance to Pacific island people. List in writing major issues for Christians in the Pacific islands and around the world, since we are one body in Christ.

Make assignments for next session. See Session 2, "Reports from Melanesia, Micronesia and Polynesia," for details.

As a brief devotional, read the Emmaus Road passage from Luke 24. Ask people to envision themselves breaking bread with a family in the Pacific. What would it be like? What might be used instead of bread? How would God be thanked and praised? How would the presence of Jesus Christ be felt?

Close with a prayer, identifying the people, leaders and concerns you have discovered in this first study session.

Session 2: Independence: People and Nations

Objectives:

1. To become familiar with the process of developing nationhood.
2. To recognize the advantages and disadvantages of colonial government.

Relevant Study Materials:

Pacific People Sing Out Strong, articles in Parts 1, 3, 4 and 5
Map 'n' Facts: Pacific Islands

Reports from Melanesia, Micronesia and Polynesia

A. At least a week in advance of the session, ask three persons to identify a country in each of the geographic sections and report on its history prior to and since independence. Besides the Coop book, sources of information include encyclopedias and magazine and newspaper articles. Consult materials in the learning resource center.

1. *Melanesia:* The Melanesian Islands cover 968,000 square kilometers, almost 90 percent of which is the island of New Guinea. Twenty-five other islands account for the remaining 10 percent. As of 1980, all the islands were independent except New Caledonia, which is still under French rule. (In the Coop book, see articles by Dr. Alexius Sarei, Bishop Gregory Singkai, Father Walter Lini, Bernard Narokobi, Sitiveni Ratuvili and Yan Celené Uregei.)

2. *Micronesia:* Over 2,000 islands are included, of which less than 100 are inhabited. Nine languages are spoken. This is a trust territory, moving to semi-independence. Be sure to identify the countries who have been "trusted" and what the results have been. (In Coop, see especially the statement by Father William T. Wood in Part V and issue articles by John Anjain and Senator Moses Uludong.)

3. *Polynesia:* These islands form a triangle from Samoa to Hawaii; from Hawaii to Easter Island; and from New Zealand to Tonga. They have a history of foreign rule, indicated by such names as French Polynesia. Tonga is the only Pacific island nation to continue to be ruled by a king.

Have each person report for approximately 10 to 15 minutes, citing information about the history, political structure and cultural patterns of the particular country. Although similarities are shared among most of the Pacific islands, differences within regional groups and even within particular cultures are important to note. Most library resources, although valuable, stop short of current political developments. Check on material published by the United Nations for recent updates, and check recent periodical and newspaper articles.

B. Ask three other persons in the group to research and report on the following concerns:

1. *Christian mission presence and its impact in the Pacific islands.* Important insights might include what it means for denominations to join in a united church through the Pacific Conference of Churches and through such churches as the United Church of Papua New Guinea and the Solomon Islands. Also, it is important to recognize that early missionary presence in Papua New Guinea came not only from Great Britain but also from Fiji; indigenous leadership was essential to the development of Christianity in the Pacific. For reference, see Part I of the Coop book. Further information on indigenous missionary work will be found in Garrett, *To Live Among the Stars* (see "Resources for This Study," chapter 1).

2. *The effect of foreign presence in Micronesia.* See, in particular, Coop's book for articles by Senator Moses Uludong and John Anjain, and the Pacific Conference of Churches Ponape Conference Report, 1978.

3. *Women in the Pacific Islands:* See the report from the Women's Conference in Suva, Fiji, 1975 in Coop.

C. In pairs, ask persons to share with each other what new information they have learned during the reports. Then, share in plenary, providing time for additional questions. If available, persons who have visited or lived in the Pacific islands would be ideal resources for this session.

An Alternative Approach

An alternative to a simple "report" session is to structure a panel discussion with six members of the group participating. An appropriate topic for discussion would be "History, Leadership and Independence in the Pacific Islands." Plan for the discussion to last for about 45 minutes, with opportunities for questions and feedback from others in the group. Questions might be about the value of North American and/or European presence in the Pacific islands; the implications of expatriate mission work with indigenous churches.

Reflection Time

Pause, having looked at the vastness of space, people, countries and issues in the Pacific islands. Think about the role of an organization like the Pacific Conference of Churches amid such diversity. The PCC brings churches together to work collaboratively on issues and theology. Listed below are its issues for the 1980s, as quoted from a PCC document:

1. *Spiritual renewal and deepening of the faith.* Rapid changes in the Pacific islands are causing people to ask questions about their faith. This is a form of Christian education.
2. *Theological education and reshaping of educational ministries.* What is the role of theological education—for clergy and for lay leaders? Both play an integral and related role in working with communities. Emphasis is away from a "hierarchical" image of the clergy.
3. *Pacific identity and solidarity.* Members of the PCC need to identify clearly who they are and work together for regional identity through dialogue and fellowship.
4. *Integral human development.* Development has been seen to be an important issue in the Pacific islands. Human development within a Christian context means such things as simultaneously helping a person earn money and teaching him/her stewardship of financial resources. Human development is related to social, not technological, development.

5. *Human rights.*
    a. Independence movement: Full independence for the island nations and removal of foreign political domination.
    b. Nuclear-free Pacific: PCC condemns the testing of nuclear bombs, the dumping of nuclear waste and the movement of nuclear weapons ships in Pacific waters.
    c. Participation of women and youth: Women and youth are seeking to be equal partners with men in decision making and free from society's traditions.
6. *Transnational corporations.* A new and emerging issue for PCC.
7. *Migration.* Movement of people within the Pacific is a concern on which PCC is working with the New Zealand Council of Churches and Christian Conference in Asia.
8. *Tourism.* Tourism is a given; maximizing its strengths and minimizing its evils are important issues.
9. *Wide gap between the rich and the poor.* The concern is that localization is becoming predominant and that national plans could be adopted for the sake of the rich, rather than inclusively. Traditional societies did not know the extreme differences in wealth that exist today.
10. *Cooperation among churches, nongovernment organizations, government and aid agencies.* Confusion arises in the islands from the lack of coordination of roles of various organizations. Working together will enable groups to provide better service to the people.

Share in open prayer based on the PCC issues. Mention each issue and allow time for participants to respond with prayer requests and intercession on behalf of these concerns.

Conclude by singing "The Voice of God is Calling," found in most hymnals.

Session 3: People of the Pacific Islands Speak About Their History and Culture

Objectives:

1. To become informed about what people of the Pacific islands say about their history and culture.

2. To recognize the importance of indigenous leadership in the Pacific islands.
3. To identify our own attitudes about Pacific island people and culture.

Relevant Study Materials:

Pacific People Sing Out Strong, Part 2
Map 'n' Facts: Pacific Islands
People of the Silver Sea (filmstrip)

Small Group Discussion

Listed on the following pages are five quotations of some length about culture, history and development in the Pacific islands. Have participants read through each one silently in plenary. When you have finished, ask each person to decide which statement he or she would like to discuss with others. Form five groups and discuss the issues raised by the quotations for approximately 20 minutes. Use the following questions to help stimulate discussion:

1. What conflicts do you see facing Pacific Islanders as they become interdependent with developed nations?
2. In what ways are the Pacific islands part of the Third World? In what ways are they not?
3. What advantages and disadvantages do you see for Pacific Islanders in development?
4. If you were a development officer with a multinational corporation assigned to one of the Pacific islands, what kind of resistance might you expect to meet? How would you want to work with the people to accomplish your task?
5. What (following #4) ways would you choose, if any, to share the culture of the Pacific islands with the corporate officers not present in your work area?
6. What do you feel North Americans have to learn from Pacific Islanders about family? About attitudes toward money? About self-esteem? About poverty? Other?

1. From **Into the Future: Development the Pacific Way**
by Ati George Sokomanu, President of Vanuatu

Development is a word that could sometimes be too highly emphasized or so overworked that one wonders whether one should not change it. Sometimes it is too lightly taken by many people in the Pacific, but it is the ultimate heart of existence and progress. We need to improve the quality of life of our people, to be self-reliant in food and to replace imports, to earn foreign exchange and to generate greater national wealth....

...There is a need for the Pacific as a region to play its part in the world community with proper and accepted terms, but more so to see regional bodies that already exist to be strengthened, socially, economically and politically.... The voice of the Pacific region must be as one to protect its people from outside exploitation, from nuclear tests, from those who come disguised as the second Messiah. Let the Pacific region develop, in the way in which its people see fit and acceptable, and this is the only way in which it can be free from strains and influences from outside that are harmful....

2. From **The Pacific Way,** *Ron Crocombe*

...The colonial experience left a common unpleasant taste in the mouths of island people: a common humiliation, a common feeling of deprivation and exploitation. It is to be hoped that The Pacific Way will not become too much a reaction of bitterness or negativeness, blaming all the difficulties of today on the errors of the past. For if it does, little creative action will be taken to resolve problems for the future, and The Pacific Way will become a way of whining dependency. The likelihood is not great, for the statement of the Pacific rises above the temptation, but the possibility is sufficiently unpleasant to need active avoidance. The new dependency, under multinational corporations and governments which provide "aid," may of course become worse than the old colonial relationship. Only time will tell.

3. *From* **Rituals of Planning and Realities of Development**
by Jone Dakuvula, graduate of the University of the South Pacific and editor of the student newspaper, UNISPAC

...Most of us assume "development" to be, if not good, at least inevitable. Development as a concept has to do with our view of "the good life." The unquestioned view of "the good life" underlying all planning today is the secular world vision where specialized technology, specialized labour, merit system and achievement orientation are the central, determinant values of human interaction. It is taken for granted that only in a secular world can our people achieve dignity, identity and solidarity. The lingering rationalities of our old societies are viewed instrumentally by planners as either "aids" or "obstacles" to achieving "development." Most social scientists are unconscious vectors of this view of "the good life." Though we may deny it, we are part of the elite who pave the way for political manipulation. By undertaking the sort of work we are doing now—defining the so-called "social issues"—we prepare the way for planners to induce value changes amongst the population. Hence, studies of people inevitably lead to manipulation.

4. From **Is Kinship Costly?** *by Nacanieli Rika, a graduate of the University of the South Pacific and principal of Lelean Memorial School in Fiji*

...When my brother died suddenly early last month, I was in the middle of my final exams....When I enquired from Administration what would happen if I was late back from the funeral (which meant a trip to Taveuni and the uncertainty of getting a return seat on the holiday weekend), I was advised by a gentleman I shall not name that examinations were more important than dead kinsmen. He further assured me that had my brother been able to give an opinion, he would have wanted me to put my exams before his funeral. I thanked him for his wise counsel and flew to Taveuni regardless....This bond of kinship descended on me in a way it had never done before. My duties and kinship obligation to my brother, and my responsibility to his widow and three small daughters, weighed heavily on me. There was no doubt in my mind as to which should come first. Two hours after I was advised not to go, I was aboard a flight bound for Matei, Taveuni.

5. From **Decolonizing and Recolonizing: The Case of the Solomon Islands** *by Francis Bogutu, Permanent Secretary for Education and Cultural Affairs for the Solomon Islands*

...The challenge for us Pacific Islanders is not to stand wide-eyed at one side of the arena, blankly watching our interests being manipulated and aspirations changed by foreigners, but to stand in the centre of the ring....The task is to find a design for a future which serves our interests, and need not necessarily be patterned on western lines, nor serve western strategic, economic or political aims....

We must have faith in ourselves and our cultures. It would be unconventional in the modern world to base any future development of an emerging nation on its own "simple" culture. Nevertheless, if we Pacific Islanders believe otherwise, we should not be deterred from building our future on what we know and understand well. One way to start looking past the new darkness brought about by the dazzling lights of civilization is to outline some strengths of one traditional way of life on which programmes of modernization could be carried out....

When you have completed discussion in small groups, reconvene and share your perspectives in plenary. Ask one person from each group to summarize the discussion. Other members may feel free to add if they feel an important perspective was omitted.

Clarifying Our Values About the Emerging Pacific

Write each of the following statements on a separate sheet of newsprint and place the sheets at different points in the room.

1. "Freedom is in fact development, whether material progress and wealth are realized to the extent expected or not." *Francis Bogutu*
2. "...the essentials for survival are not just material; also important is the maintenance of a sense of identity, solidarity, and dignity." *Jone Dakuvula*
3. "If freedom to examine and criticize is not guaranteed in our Pacific societies, then we will have failed in one of the most important preconditions of dealing humanely with human problems." *Jone Dakuvula*
4. "As we embark on development schemes to modernize our communities and societies, what should be valued more: a materially affluent society with a high per capita income devoid of human feelings, or a society that is not so affluent but places great value on its humanity, and on forging human bonds?" *Nacanieli Rika*

Read the statements aloud in the group, or allow time for people to move around the room and read the statements. The purpose of this exercise is to discover our attitudes about development issues in the Pacific islands. People are to pick the statement to which they respond most strongly, either positively or negatively. They should then find the newsprint sheet with that statement on it and clarify with one another their individual feelings about the statement. This is not a time to argue or try to convince someone about the validity of your own opinion. Every opinion is valid in its own right. After spending 10 minutes at one sheet, ask people to move to another statement that impressed them and continue the process until all members have had a chance to discuss each statement.

In plenary, when the rotation is completed, focus on the following questions:

- What did you learn about your own attitudes? Are you satisfied? Could you be more satisfied?
- Were you surprised by the responses of others?
- What relationship does development have to your work in this country? To your relationship with your family? Your church?
- What opportunities does your denomination provide for self-development in this country or around the world? Do you think this is a good idea? Why or why not?

Invite people to add their own statements for the group to react to, based on their own experience and set of beliefs. Examples might be:

- Development in the Pacific islands is to be avoided at all costs.
- Self-determination means less involvement from European and western countries.
- Providing financial assistance to indigenous churches may not encourage them to be as self-supporting as possible.
- Sending missionaries to the Pacific islands was important; but they should have left the islands sooner!

Additional Activities

Those who are interested in learning about the cultures of the Pacific in greater detail may want to work on additional or alternative projects in this session. See the suggestions under "Interest Areas" in chapter 1 for ideas, and use your learning resource center.

The filmstrip *People of the Silver Sea* gives insight, through pictures, words and music, into the cultures and lifestyles of the Pacific people. Arrange a viewing and suggest that participants pay special attention to the importance of land and sea on human life, to the variety of art and craft forms, to the relative importance of people versus things and to conflicts between traditional values and modern ways of living.

An understanding of the music, arts and crafts, foods, customs and values of the islands is basic to an understanding of the people themselves.

Reflection Time

Read aloud the prayer "Our Pacific Islands" by Bernard Narokobi, found at the beginning of *Pacific People Sing Out Strong*. Ask members of the group to reflect on it in their own shared prayer.

Session 4: Stewardship: A Biblical and Cultural Issue

Objectives:

1. To discover the depth of stewardship as a practice of the Pacific island peoples.
2. To explore the meanings of stewardship in our own experience, and to identify similarities and differences between North American perspectives and those of the Pacific islands.

Relevant Study Materials:

Pacific People Sing Out Strong, "Concerning the Pacific" in Part 1; Part 6

Opening Activity

In plenary, identify all the meanings of *stewardship* the group can think of, and have someone write them on newsprint. Take about 5 to 10 minutes for this, depending on the size of the group. When you have exhausted the group's ideas, ask people to identify quickly what they consider to be the stewardship activities of their congregation. Is this list similar to the first one? In what ways might stewardship, in its broadest sense, be expanded in the practice of most congregations?

Small Group Discussion

Ask members to divide into groups of four or five persons each. Take 20 minutes to discuss reactions to and insights about one of the following quotes:

1. The Pacific seems to live up to its name. . . . This raises fundamental human rights questions. (From "Concerning the Pacific," page 12, *Pacific People Sing Out Strong.*)
2. Reviving Traditional Culture in Fiji. Western Culture forced its way into Fiji through personnel, business, communication media, and so on. This culture brought things both helpful and unhelpful. Two obvious things are capitalism and freedom, which were enforced in the education system in Fiji and became the objectives of education. People in Fiji were not well acquainted with these ideas or how to use them.

The result is that people in Fiji, especially Fijians, are confused and disappointed. They tend to think the major goal of education is MONEY—to get a job to earn money. Failure in examinations means failure in life. The whole attitude to life is to focus on capitalism, the winning of money. If people have no money, they feel they cannot cope with life. . . . In Lau, chiefs have formed a council to revive the traditional culture. They have aimed to strengthen the traditional social structure, provide an environment for cultural education and decrease the demand for money. (From *Shaping Educational Ministry*, published by Lotu Pasifika Productions, Suva, Fiji, 1977.)
3. French colonial presence in the Pacific. . . . No situation in the Pacific calls for more immediate and sensitive attention than New Caledonia. (From "Concerning the Pacific," page 13, *Pacific People Sing Out Strong.*)
4. Concerning Stewardship. . . . We must learn to deal humbly and responsibly at every stage with our limitations. (From "Concerning the Pacific," page 14, *Pacific People Sing Out Strong.*)

As the groups discuss these quotations, they should address the following questions and issues:
1. Are the ideas of stewardship or related concepts that are identified in the quotations similar/dissimilar to those on the lists made earlier in the session? In what ways?
2. In quotation 1, what are the human rights questions referred to at the end of the statement?
3. In quotation 2, is the concept of capitalism, as reinforced by the educational system, destined always to be related to money? How could it be otherwise? How could it be otherwise in our own North American culture?
4. In quotation 3, how is the situation described a form of genocide? The authors of the statement call for prompt atten-

tion to the situation in New Caledonia. What kind of attention might be appropriate, in keeping with a broad concept of stewardship?
5. In quotation 4, what form would accountability to future generations (as a form of stewardship) take in the Pacific islands? How might the Pacific Conference of Churches help to enable such accountability?

Come together in plenary session for a brief period of sharing. Follow the procedure of earlier sessions by having a reporter from each small group, with members being free to comment or add information.

Bible Study

Divide into different small groups for Bible study. Read the following passages of Scripture: Genesis 1:20-29; Psalm 8:1-9; Micah 6:6-8; Matthew 6:24-27; Matthew 14:13-21; Luke 10:25-27; 2 Corinthians 8:1-5. Each of these passages reflects a different interpretation of what God does through us or for us or expects from us. Discuss the following questions:
- What kind of stewardship does God expect of you?
- As a receiver of God's (and others') gifts, how might you appropriately respond?
- What are the tangible signs of God's provision in your life? How does the way you respond reflect an attitude about stewardship?
- Based on what you have learned about the Pacific islands and their people, what responses might they have to these passages?

Reflection Time

Read Psalm 8 aloud as a closing reflection. Invite people to respond with their own thoughts.

Session 5: The Vision: A Nuclear-Free Pacific

Objectives:

1. To clarify our values about nuclear proliferation in the Pacific.
2. To become informed about the reasons the Pacific Conference of Churches has identified a nuclear-free Pacific as a top priority.

3. To develop awareness of nuclear-related issues in the Pacific for future reference.

Relevant Study Materials:

Pacific People Sing Out Strong, Parts 3 and 5
Map 'n' Facts: Pacific Islands
People of the Silver Sea
Current periodical and newspaper clippings from your learning resource center

Clarifying Attitudes*

The purpose of this activity is to clarify our positions about nuclear involvement in the Pacific. We have already discovered facts and issues related to the culture, the value of land and people's interdependence with it, and self-government and transitions from colonial rule. What we have already done will inform us as we respond to this activity.

Place a strip of masking tape on the floor of your meeting place. At each end of the tape, place a card with one of the following statements:

Nuclear development in the Pacific islands is a necessary activity to assure "global peace."

Nuclear development is a threat to the culture and human rights of people in the Pacific islands and should be stopped immediately.

Ask people to imagine that the tape is a continuum. The continuum has two poles which reflect different attitudes and values about nuclear development in the Pacific islands. The cards represent these two poles.

Read the two statements aloud. Ask participants to think about them for a few moments, and then to take a position on the continuum which represents their belief about this issue.

When everyone has taken a position, take a look at where other people are and where you are. Give persons five minutes to go to another participant who is standing somewhere else on the continuum and try to convince him/her to move in a different direction toward another position.

*This exercise is a variation of one used by Sidney Simon in his book *Values Clarification* (New York: A & W Pubs., Inc., rev. ed. 1978).

At the conclusion of the interaction time, ask people to move to the position which *at the present moment* most accurately represents their positions. Ask people to indicate if they moved from the first point in the activity. If so, why? What factors were influential? What additional information do they need, or wish to have? Were there any surprises about the positions of other people in the group? What additional conversation is necessary to clarify positions and attitudes? What histories, if any, do participants have of factors such as World War II fighting in the Pacific, which influence their positions on this issue? What broader issues about nuclear development, not limited to the Pacific islands, have been raised for further consideration?

A Statement from the PCC

In addition to the articles in the Coop book (particularly those by John Anjain, Senator Moses Uludong, Father William T. Wood, and the Pacific Conference of Churches report on the Ponape Conference), the following comments were prepared by the Pacific Conference of Churches. Read through the statement, making note of the issues of nuclear technology which the PCC sees as crucial and perhaps unique for the Pacific islands.

Resolutions and statements on nuclear issues have been put forward regularly by the Pacific churches since 1974. A special commission was directed by the Pacific Conference of Churches to the U.N. Special Session on Disarmament in 1978. Again, representatives of the Pacific churches in a world Christian meeting held in Melbourne in May of this year [1980] issued a strongly-worded statement. It protested nuclear testing in the Pacific; the proliferation of nuclear weapons; the testing of ballistic missiles designed to carry nuclear warheads; the dumping of nuclear wastes; and the deployment of nuclear-powered ships and submarines.

So the debate goes on. Meanwhile, the powerful custodians of nuclear technology continue to make the crucial choices, laying out courses of action with frightening long-term implications.

The past two to three years has been an extremely significant period for those thoughtfully weighing questions of nuclear technology. Nuclear accidents, recently available results of studies on the effects of radiation, clarification of the economics of nuclear power, and a growing number of dissenting professionals have greatly enriched the global experience.

There is no worthy life without risk, but do the benefits justify the risks? The effect of radiation upon human beings and other living things is at the heart of the risk-benefit issue for nuclear technology. We have therefore included several readings dealing with the effect of radiation upon persons.

Experience is now demonstrating that the effect of radiation is more serious than earlier believed. Studies now suggest that *no* level of radiation is safe, that the effect of radiation is cumulative. "Permissible level" standards are being revised downwards. While there is admittedly natural radiation in our environment, some of it harmful, this should not be confused with the nature, scale, and potential consequences of human-made radiation.

More and more professionals are saying that we do not have a sound technical basis for the responsible disposal of nuclear wastes. At the same time, whether we like it or not, there *are* radioactive wastes, and in substantial amounts (relative to the danger involved).

There is a point of view, therefore, which says that a "safer" place must be identified and *accepted* for the disposal of nuclear wastes, or else we will have more and more accidents and more nations going to the dangerous procedure called "reprocessing." It is generally accepted that reprocessing will result in a frightening proliferation of weapons grade materials.

Others say that we must not allow those creating radioactive wastes to take this easy way out! All nuclear fission technologies are a potential basis for nuclear violence and coercion, not to mention catastrophic accidents or subversion. We cannot put radioactive wastes away, because *there is no "Away!"* We know of no practicable means to erase the radioactivity, and we have no way of ensuring the vigilance of a thousand years. We must not compromise our active resistance to those who would create more wastes until we have a clear technical and socio-political basis for doing so.

Taking this position is not to "demonize" technology, nor is it to demand that technology solve all its problems before encountering them! It is to say that we now have enough experience to conclude that we are dealing with a very special case, that for this case it is time to "de-progress" until we *do* clearly have a technical and socio-political basis to progress.

Some writers have suggested that nuclear power is at the crossroads of its own survival. It is their claim that for fundamental reasons, the commercial viability of nuclear power is under serious question, that only in centrally planned economies is bureaucratic power sufficient to override the economic realities. They say that the "collapse" of nuclear power in response to the market place is to be welcomed, as the nuclear power industry is the driving force behind nuclear proliferation; is an ineffective way to replace oil, is retarding oil power displacement by diverting attention away from other important options.

When the scientists differ, then the rest of us are most perplexed! Thank God that the debate among scientists on this issue is increasingly open! Let us interpret the stated opinions of technical people and officials through the perspective of their vested interests. Is nuclear technology being swept forward by a momentum of its own which is overriding human values? If so, then let it be braked. This area of technology (and perhaps all others?) should go forward only through thoughtful, deliberate choice....

Some Proposed Theological Themes

Surely a most special and important role for the churches to play in this continuing and sacramental dialogue is to continually raise questions in relation to their biblical/theological base. Some basic theological themes come to mind for exploration and reflection:

1. The sanctity of life and our stewardship of the created order; our solemn responsibility to all humankind, including future generations;
2. The "finitude" (the limited nature) of humans and of earth: the limited cleverness of human beings and the limited capacity of the earth to suffer exploitation;
3. The intimate, integral relationship between human beings and nature. Is the modern, industrial and technological civilisation driving a wedge, causing a split, between humanity and nature?
4. What is "authentic human development"? What is the "Good Life"? What does it mean to be fully human? What is a "good society"? What forms of human life-style best express and support the profound meanings of life?
5. Justice in relationships between nations, between regions, between generations;
6. How do we confront the reality of Sin? Not only the arrogance, greed and broken relationships of individuals, but also the structural, the institutional sin which puts the narrow national or corporate self-interest ahead of all other considerations. How shall we as a Pacific community responsibly relate to such a frustrating, difficult, but critically important task?

7. The challenge for humankind in its brokenness to take risks for peace. With the realities of the 1980s and beyond as a frame of reference, what is "good thinking," or thinking which tries to consider the totality of relationships (the Bible uses the term "metanoia")? How may we contribute to dialogue leading toward new peace dynamics in the world, toward a de-escalation of the fear and mistrust which has the world locked into an insane armaments and energy race?

Specific biblical references have intentionally been omitted. We hope that some of our readers and their groups might be willing to explore with us these and other themes in relation to specific biblical passages.

B. David Williams Jr., Coordinator
Church and Society Program
Pacific Conference of Churches
Suva, September 1980

Choose one or two of the questions posed at the end of this statement for brief plenary discussion. Assuming there are differences of opinion and attitude in the group, do not attempt to come to a consensus unless the group wishes to do so. It is important for everyone to feel free to speak about their attitudes and to feel "heard" by the rest of the group.

Reflection Time

Show the last portion of the filmstrip *People of the Silver Sea*, beginning with frame 77. This portion will leave the group with several ideas to reflect on.

Close the session with prayer:

A Prayer for the Church

O God our creator, we pray for the Church, which is set today in the midst of the confusion and difficult choices of a rapidly changing world, a Church face to face with so many new and bewildering tasks.

We pray that you will baptise her anew with the life-giving spirit of Jesus! May she be utterly loyal to your will, proclaiming the truth boldly in love, in the great tradition of your prophets.

Fill her with Christlike concern for justice, stewardship and peacemaking. May she not fall to the temptation of seeking her own life, lest she lose it, but be brave to put out her life for

humanity—so that like her crucified Lord she may go forward by the pathway of the Cross to a higher glory. Amen.
—*Prepared by the Pacific Conference of Churches*

Session 6: Participants in a Global Community: Personal Involvement

Objectives:

1. To discover opportunities for personal involvement.
2. To explore attitudes about mission and how Christians around the world are interrelated and interdependent.

Relevant Study Materials:

Pacific People Sing Out Strong, especially Part 6
Map 'n' Facts: Pacific Islands
People of the Silver Sea
Current material from the learning resource center

Small Group Discussion

Challenges from the Pacific

Have all participants read "The Challenges of the 1980s and the Pacific Churches" by Leslie Boseto, in *Pacific People Sing Out Strong.* Boseto addresses not only the social and political issues facing the Pacific islands, but also faces openly the issues set forth by the Pacific Conference of Churches.

In small groups of about five people each, respond to the following questions:

1. Boseto says that Moses "preferred to suffer with God's people rather than to enjoy sin for a little while." What implications does this have for Pacific island people?
2. Boseto talks about the kingdom of God being present "with us" not through the work of theologians, but through communal solidarity. What do you think he means by this? What implications does this have for the North American church?
3. The importance of the local church to national governments is crucial for Boseto. What knowledge do you have of the ways in

which the church, nationally, is involved in the leadership of the Pacific island nations? What role might or could the Pacific Conference of Churches play in bringing together a variety of national issues?

After about 15 to 20 minutes in small groups, ask one person from each group to report on the discussion. In plenary, discuss the following issues.

Dr. Sioni A. Havea comments in an article "Church Unity in Diversity in the Pacific" that "the Pacific Conference of Churches is not a church, nor does it wish to regard itself as one." What advantages does the PCC have in being not a single church but rather a fellowship of churches?

The PCC sees its unity as a strength as it plays a prophetic role in its approach to justice and human rights issues, according to Havea. In what ways does the denomination or church of which you are a member participate in organizations which strengthen its capacity to be prophetic? How might your church be further involved in interchurch efforts?

Assumptions About Mission

Below is a list of assumptions North American Christians may hold about mission.* Mark an "A" for agree and "D" for disagree beside the statements.

1. Mission is a program for us to implement.
2. The United States experience of development, both in nation and in church, is a model for other churches around the world.
3. No one completely understands the gospel. It is offered to all people. Our continued openness to the gospel is part of our witness to it.
4. We can agree ahead of time on the reasons and methods of our mission and must do so if we are to talk about a mandate for mission.
5. Mission is a gift from God.
6. Mission is what we do "for the good of others."
7. Mission announces that the kingdom of God is at hand.
8. Mission is aimed at changing others; encouraging them to give up cultural patterns for a "broader view."
9. Mission is the story of God's saving activity in which we are privileged to take part.

*These statements are adapted from an article appearing in *A.D.* Magazine, October 1978.

10. Mission happens only as we are open and sensitive to God's action in the world.
11. Mission looks to the future.
12. Mission is involved with persons.
13. Mission is aimed at getting results.
14. The United States experience is today more a problem to the rest of the world than a model. Today's need in all parts of the world church is to be open to the perspective and critique of other parts.
15. Serious involvement with persons who have perspectives and experiences different from our own always brings surprises. Openness to these surprises is part of taking part in God's history.
16. Mission depends on financial support.
17. We can be confident in our mission program.
18. Involvement with others raises questions of whether we know what is good for others and for ourselves as well.
19. The mission task is pretty much the same everywhere in the world.
20. The experiences of mission require us to reflect on our reasons and our methods, and often to live with tension as we are forced to change our minds.
21. Mission is a program that we know how to describe and carry out.
22. Mission depends on God's spirit.
23. The mission task develops in concrete situations. Our witness is shaped as we enter them.
24. We appear differently to others. Self-understanding and self-deception often overlap.

In small groups, pick three statements that can be substantiated by your study of the Pacific islands and their people. One person should be prepared to share these in the entire group. Take about 15 minutes for this portion of the exercise.

In plenary, share as many different statements and learnings about the Pacific islands as the group is able to generate.

Ongoing Projects

Consider one or more of the following for your congregation:
1. Subscribe to a United Nations magazine to broaden readers' picture of world interdependence. Put it in your church library.

2. Use 1982 (or part of 1983) as a year to focus your congregation's awareness on the Pacific islands. Try some of the following activities:
   a. Place *Map 'n' Facts: Pacific Islands* on a bulletin board in the narthex or another well-traveled place in your church. Place at least one current news item per week related to the Pacific on the board. Use colored yarn to relate news articles to the country being mentioned. If your congregation/denomination knows of personnel serving in that country, indicate their names and secure pictures of them for the bulletin board.
   b. Schedule a "Minute for Mission" on the Pacific islands at least once a month.
   c. Use World-Wide Communion Sunday (the first Sunday in October) to focus on the global community of the church, including the Pacific islands.
   d. Create an adult study series, adapted to your time frame, using the material in this study guide and your learning resource center. Or keep your learning resource center ongoing and add to it.
3. Consider writing letters to your United Nations representative (and your president or prime minister), or representatives of other countries, expressing your convictions about nuclear development and testing in the Pacific islands.

An Intergenerational Celebration

Children's groups in your church are probably also engaged in a study of the Pacific islands. Their explorations will concentrate on cultural aspects of life in the Pacific rather than on major global issues such as nuclear testing, and sharing in their work can help adults to achieve a deeper understanding of these aspects.

Detailed instructions for an intergenerational celebration are included in chapter 4 of this guide, "Children Experience the Pacific Islands." You will want to plan ways to use *Map 'n' Facts* and the filmstrip in your celebration. Materials from the learning resource center and projects that group members may have done in Session 3 or at other points in the study can be shared at this time.

Remember that celebration is important to Pacific people. Perhaps we North Americans can learn as much from this attitude to life as from some of the difficult issues confronting Pacific peoples today.

Reflection Time

Share prayers of thanksgiving and intercession for persons, cultures, nations and churches in the Pacific islands. Base your prayers on learned experience through the study you have completed.

Close with the reading of Matthew 25:14–30, the parable of the talents. Discuss new meanings this parable might have as the result of understanding "talents" as more than a financial unit. What implications does this have for shared ministry with the Pacific islands in the way Boseto described?

4. Children Experience the Pacific Islands

Global Education for Children: What and Why

One of the most important reasons for children to learn about the Pacific islands and their people is *family.* In chapter 3, Session 3 of this guide, you read a statement about kinship. Kinship and family in Pacific island cultures refer not merely to bloodlines, but also to an extended family which is part of a child's world. The *nuclear family* of parents and children, as North Americans understand it, is simply not relevant in and of itself to the cultural patterns in the Pacific. Rather, *extended families* and communities as families provide a much larger understanding of community and interdependence.

Related to the concept of family is the variety of ways in which children are nurtured in the Pacific islands. Because illiteracy is a significant issue, family education is of primary importance. Regardless of formal education, the family and its education into the cultural patterns and values of society remains a priority. Two examples from Papua New Guinea illustrate the nature of family life:

1. Children often are not disciplined by their parents. In fact, in many communities, it is assumed that children are gifts to be enjoyed and that to curtail their activities — to redirect their energies (in Western educational psychology) — is to be an unfaithful parent. Thus a 5-year-old may use a tape cassette player and break it and the parent will simply report it as fact, with no thought of removing such equipment from a youngster's reach!
2. A second example is the way theological education is pursued at Rarongo Theological College, the seminary of the United

Church of Papua New Guinea and the Solomon Islands. Housing accommodations for students are largely family quarters. Students are expected to come to the seminary for a five-year course of study. It is never assumed that such training will precede marriage and family life; rather, the two are integrally related.

Increasingly, North American children will be living in a globally interdependent world. The complexities of the distribution of the world's resources will increasingly be a part of their lives. The oil crunch of the 1970s, for example, made children aware that the gasoline they took for granted was not an "American" resource, but one which we shared with others around the world (and then, disproportionately). Although we are not physically dependent on the Pacific islands for natural resources, the political relationships among countries in the Pacific, and between those countries and others in the world, promises to shape the world in which children will be living 20 to 50 years from today.

It is appropriate for children to discover the advantages and disadvantages of colonial development. Although children cannot understand all the complexities of colonial development, they might be helped to develop a role play situation in which one group is indigenous people, and the other group or groups Europeans or North Americans who have come to use the first group's resources and try to change their way of life. Such an experience would provide a simple context in which children could come to understand why countries have changed their names, wanted different national leadership, and so forth.

It is to be hoped that children will develop an attitude of openness to and appreciation for the world in which they live that will stay with them in the years ahead. They can learn to understand that responsible relationships around the world may not mean "taking care of" a less-developed nation, but instead coming to understand important things about the way people live and what we can learn from them. The activities for children will attempt to expand the possibilities for helping children understand "global education."

Preparing to Teach

Before the sessions begin, the members of the teaching team will need to spend some time familiarizing themselves with the materials for the course and with the Pacific in general. The basic resources for children, which are described in detail in chapter 1 of this guide, are:

Follow the Sun..., by Gweneth Deverell (5 story papers for early elementaries)

Come to My Place: Meet My Island Family, stories from the Pacific compiled by Esiteri Kamikamica (for older elementaries)

Map 'n' Facts: Pacific Islands

People of the Silver Sea, filmstrip; frames 1-37, with special script and soundtrack, constitute the children's portion.

In addition, teachers should read the basic adult study book, *Pacific People Sing Out Strong,* by William Coop. This will provide valuable background information. Read through this guide in its entirety, also, and be alert to news reports and periodical articles about the area.

Teachers also need to know as much as possible about the children who will be in the class. Try to phone or drop a note to each before the sessions begin, saying that you are looking forward to having him or her in your class and perhaps mentioning briefly something you will be doing.

If you plan to use the learning resource center approach, you will need to begin gathering materials as soon as possible. The center may be part of the larger adult one, used intergenerationally. In this case, be sure it can be readily accessible to children during the course of this study. In some settings, children will have to be taught how to use the learning center. It is important to have enough resource people to help children continue the learning process and to answer questions. If the center is set up in such a way that children can do specific activities in specific locations, you will need to have at least one resource person for each activity.

The Learning Resource Center and Alternative Methods

One of the primary advantages of a learning resource center is that it is individualized. That is, it allows different children to learn at various levels, in various ways, and with varying degrees of enthusiasm! Plan for flexibility in your use of resources and be prepared for children to respond at their levels of interest. Always be ready to stimulate the quick learner with other activities. Using his or her enthusiasm may be a way to motivate others.

Learning resource centers need not be highly complex. A simple learning center for this study might include the following items:

1. *Map 'n' Facts: Pacific Islands* with names of countries clearly labeled.
2. Books or pictures of the Pacific islands and their people. Even photocopied pages from encyclopedias which summarize information in children's language would be useful.
3. A food display. One session might include sampling a variety of fruits from the Pacific. Ask children to see if they can find the fruits and bring them in (or bring in pictures if the fruits are not readily available). The list might include bananas, coconuts, mangoes, and so forth.
4. A work area, with construction paper, crayons, paints and a variety of art materials. Supplies can be accumulated when you have decided what types of projects you will suggest to the children.

The learning center could also be a place where children know they can come at the beginning of a session to explore what is new, to add items, to reinvestigate something from the week before. Invite children to add to the learning center by bringing in pictures they may have found or dolls they may have at home. Children may benefit from simply having a place where they can work independently and where the focus of this unit of study will be.

You might wish to use the learning center for some of the following activities related to *Follow the Sun* and *Come to My Place:*

- Keep the ongoing vocabulary list here so that children can add to it on a regular basis.
- If children make the Big Books suggested in *Follow the Sun,* the learning center could be a place to store them from week to week.
- Have children pick a name for themselves from the list "What's In a Name?" in *Come to My Place* and print it on a tag, strung with string, and wear it for a portion of the study activities.
- Have children draw pictures to illustrate a scene in one of the story papers or a story in *Come to My Place.* Hang the pictures on the wall and ask several children to describe what they have drawn and what happened in the story.

The learning resource center allows you to offer the group a choice of several activities at a time. An alternative approach would be to select one or two activities for each session. (Some suggestions for activities are in the next section of this guide.) Such an approach might mean, for example, drawing pictures one week and taking them home, or placing them in the hallway instead of the classroom. Or children might take the name tags home instead of leaving them in the center. The activities suggested for the learning resource center can be constructed in other areas for the study.

The session plans included here are designed to be flexible in time frame. Depending on the size of the group and the time available, the sessions could be done partially in 30 minutes or could easily be extended to 60 minutes or longer.

Resources and Activities

Here are some ideas to help you plan meaningful learning experiences for your group. On the basis of your available time and what you know about the abilities, needs and interests of your children, pick and choose from among these. Adapt them as necessary, and use them as a starting point for some creative thinking of your own — and of the children.

*Pacific Animals, Plants and Languages**

Many different languages are spoken in the Pacific. Here are some very general pronunciation helps.
(a) The vowels:

a	as in f*a*ther	but	shortened
e	as in p*a*y	,,	,,
i	as in h*e*	,,	,,
o	as in go	,,	,,
u	as in zoo	,,	,,

(b) The consonants are pronounced as in English.
  Exceptions: Kiribati is pronounced Kiribas.
              Tahitian Iesu (Jesus) is pronounced Ietu.
              Samoan Iesu (Jesus) is pronounced Yesu.

The following checklist refers especially to the story papers but is also useful for children using *Come to My Place*.

*Based on material supplied by Gweneth Deverell, author of *Follow the Sun*.

Checklist of Animals, Plants and Pacific Island Words

	PLANTS	ANIMALS	WORDS	
Tahiti	breadfruit bananas frangipani hibiscus	chicken pigs fish	*Ia orana outou* *motu* *Te Atua* *Iesu*	— greeting — island — God — Jesus
Samoa	coconut taro bananas yams cocoa	cattle pigs poultry	*Talofa lava* *povi* *pua'a* *moa* *fa'i* *niu* *koko* *Iesu* *Atua*	— greeting — cattle — pig — poultry — banana — coconut — cocoa — Jesus — God
Fiji	damanu tree yams taro cassava bamboo	chicken turtles gulls pigs dogs crabs lingula	*Jisu* *Kalou* *ika* *tina* *vula* *wai*	— Jesus — God — fish — mother — moon — water
Vanuatu	bamboo yams bananas manioc mangoes coconut	chicken crabs	*God* *Jisas* Pidgin words are found in the song in story paper 4	— God — Jesus
Kiribati (Kiribas)	coral grass coconuts	starfish sea anemones shark fish		

*Activities**

For help in developing these and many other kinds of learning activities, see *Clues to Creativity,* vols. 1–3 (see chapter 5, "Additional Resources").

Role play. Many opportunities to learn through role play can be provided in this study. For example, some children may be the North American visitors introduced in the story papers and others

*Based on ideas provided by Doris Willis, Board of Discipleship, The United Methodist Church.

may be their Pacific island hosts and hostesses. Role play episodes from the stories in the study materials; some of the occupations mentioned; the training of church workers in the islands before they go to other islands to spread the good news.

Music. Learn the songs in the study materials. If someone can accompany the children on a guitar, this would be appropriate and fun. Drums and bells could also be used.

Storytelling. As story paper 3 points out, story*telling* rather than reading is common in the Pacific. Adults and children could learn the stories in *Follow the Sun* and *Come to My Place* so that they can retell them in their own words. Consider using simple props or gestures; put a little drama into the activity.

Handicrafts. Several types of handicrafts that children can do are suggested in the materials—making necklaces of shells, seeds or flowers; making tapa cloth, which can be used for the cover of the Big Book or for making the long skirtlike garments worn traditionally in the area; making kites and other toys suggested in *Come to My Place*; weaving floor mats.

Painting and drawing. Emphasize scenes from the stories; or suggest that children use Pacific designs in various ways. Samples of such designs are found in the study materials.

Make a village. A three-dimensional village could consist of 20 to 30 homes with a church near the center. It might be located in a valley or near the coastline. Study the artwork in *Follow the Sun* and *Come to My Place* for ideas about what the buildings should look like; get ideas from the filmstrip, *People of the Silver Sea*. You might also refer to the photos in *Pacific People Sing Out Strong*. Early elementary children might like to make the monument described in story paper 1.

Map work. Geography is an important facet of this study. Younger children might plot the course of their journey on *Map 'n' Facts,* using colored yarn, or they could pin small airplanes or boats to the map to mark different episodes in the journey. Older children could make a large table map, showing such physical characteristics as reefs, plantations, lagoons, mountains.

Collect objects from the sea. If you live near the ocean, children might spend some time exploring and collecting shells, driftwood, stones and other objects.

Have an agricultural fair. Children in a rural area could be helped to identify with Pacific island children by staging their own agricultural fair. Use pets, plants they may have grown in their gardens, handicrafts made during the sessions, tools or gardening equipment. This could be done in conjunction with story paper 2, but children from both age groups would enjoy participating.

Plan a Pacific worship service. Use music from the study materials; find ideas in "Sunday—A Special Day" in *Come to My Place;* arrange the group with girls on the left, boys on the right and choir in the middle; if safety regulations permit, have participants carry lighted candles as they enter. Use the Bible verse printed on the monument in story paper 1 in your service.

Session 1

Objective: To identify where the Pacific islands are, their geography, climate, the people.

Resources:

Follow the Sun...to Tahiti, to Western Samoa, to Fiji, to Melanesia, to Micronesia
Come to My Place: Meet My Island Family
Map 'n' Facts: Pacific Islands
People of the Silver Sea

Introduction

Have the *Map 'n' Facts: Pacific Islands* prominently posted in the room or in the learning center. Ask the children if they know where the Pacific Ocean is. Do they know the names of any countries in the Pacific islands? (Hawaii is not a country!) Continue the discussion for several minutes and introduce the study unit. Tell them why you are choosing to study the Pacific islands and share with them at least one thing you want them to learn as the result of your study together. Some possible objectives might include the following:
- to learn more about one country in the Pacific
- to learn how the people in the Pacific islands live
- to learn about the church in the Pacific islands
- to eat some of the foods of people in the Pacific islands

- to discover something about the education of children in the Pacific islands.

Introduce the study materials. If possible, have one set of story papers or one copy of *Come to My Place* for each child. Suggest some possible activities for the course and try to get an idea of what appeals most to the children.

Viewing the Filmstrip

Preview *People of the Silver Sea* prior to class time. Before beginning your viewing, ask the children to be watching for new things about the Pacific islands. After the filmstrip is concluded, ask them to work with one other person to answer the following questions:

1. Name one thing children do with their families. (*plant crops for food*)
2. Name one animal that we sometimes have for a pet that is common in the Pacific Ocean. (*turtle*)
3. Describe how people came to learn about Jesus Christ. (*from Pacific Islanders who were missionaries from Tahiti, Cook Islands and Tonga*)
4. What do the names Polynesia, Melanesia and Micronesia describe (*areas where people are more alike in their customs, looks, languages*)

Children who read well might wish to work with these additional questions (answers to these questions can be found in the filmstrip or *Map 'n' Facts*):

5. What are the names of three countries and their capital cities?
6. What do the people look like? Why do you think they dress the way they do in the film?
7. Name one person who explored the Pacific islands.
8. What is one issue facing the people in the future?
9. Name one European country which has governed part of the Pacific islands in the past.
10. List one "old name" and one "new name" for a country in the Pacific islands. (*New Hebrides/Vanuatu; Ellis Islands/Tuvalu; Gilbert Islands/Kiribati*)

Follow-up Activity

In conclusion, ask children to list as many new things as they can think of that they learned. Write them down on newsprint for future reference and to use as a review in opening the next session.

Session 2

Objective: To become acquainted with cultural patterns of Pacific island people.

Resources:

Follow the Sun... to Tahiti
Come to My Place
Map 'n' Facts: Pacific Islands
Pictures from magazines, travel agencies, etc. of the Pacific islands
Fruit representative of the Pacific islands — coconut, bananas, mangoes, pineapples

Introduction

Review with the children the things they listed in the follow-up activity at the end of the previous session. Do they have new questions? Do they need to review the map or a portion of the filmstrip?

For Younger Children

Using story paper 1 in *Follow the Sun,* invite children to participate in looking at the picture of the monument and answer the questions listed. Discuss the Bible verse on the monument (John 3:16). What might be some reasons for putting this verse on the monument?

Divide the group in half and have one group work on making flower necklaces and the other group begin a Big Book about the journey. When the book cover is complete, engage the class in a discussion about what kinds of things they will want to include in the book as they continue their study of the Pacific islands.

For Older Children

Select in advance one of the stories in *Come to My Place* and read it through. Have children role play the story as they see it. Be ready with any necessary or available props. When the children have completed the role play, ask them to describe how they felt playing different characters.

As you select a story, keep in mind the following questions for focusing discussion:

1. "Carry the Cat"
   What similarities do you find in the ways children act in Papua New Guinea and in North America?
   Describe what you think the "bush" looks like. What dangers might Luke have found there?
2. "Sene and the School Banner"
   List all the ways you remember that Sene used things around her to make the necklace.
   Does $1.20 seem like very little money for material for a new dress?
   What does that tell you about how much people make for a living?
   What did you learn about Sene's family?
3. "Manoa's Fishing Trip"
   What did you learn about relationships in this Fijian family?
   What did Manoa and his uncle hope to catch during their trip?
   What would they do with their catch?
   In what ways do things grown in North America, and particularly near where you live, become part of the food you eat?
4. "The New Canoe"
   What are the two primary ways people travel in this story?
   What did you learn about how people "pay" for goods and services?
   If you don't already know what *taro* means, look it up in a dictionary. What might you have eaten in your home that was something like taro?
5. "The Calling of the Turtles"
   Why do you think people in the Solomon Islands have legends?
   Tell a legend you know about something in North America.

Follow-up Activity

Talk briefly about each of the fruits brought in for today's session and ways they might be used in North America. Some of the fruits will be more familiar to the children than others. Invite children to sample each fruit. Such fruits are usually part of the daily diet of Pacific island children.

Session 3

Objective: To learn about similar kinds of experiences shared by children in the Pacific islands and in North America.

Resources:

Follow the Sun... to Melanesia
Come to My Place
Map 'n' Facts

Introduction

Ask the children to think about things they do every day that they think children in other parts of the world, particularly the Pacific islands, also do. They may respond with such suggestions as: go to school, help around the house, play with animals, and so forth. Tell them that today you will be thinking about some ways in which they are similar to and different from children in the Pacific islands.

For Younger Children

Read with the children the story about Tasale from Vanuatu. Ask them to listen for things in Tasale's life that are similar to their own, as well as things and activities that are different. If you wish to augment the information on education, see the material in *Come to My Place* on "Children at Home, School and Play." Paraphrase this information as you tell the children about other places in the Pacific islands.

Help children identify ways in which they are similar to Pacific island children. Ask them how they would describe something about their own school or life at home to these children. Invite them to draw a picture about Tasale which could be put in the Big Book.

Ask children who are good readers to read through the words to the song "Go Olraoni". Point out the pidgin language and ask them to find similarities between the English and pidgin words.

For Older Children

Ask children to read through the material in *Come to My Place* on children at home, school and play. What similarities are there between their own experiences and those of these children? Describe them. What in the material they have read seems like something they would enjoy about the Pacific islands? Why? What would they find difficult about living on an island?

Have them select one of the games described in the reading material and play that game as a group.

Follow-up Activity

Ask for three older elementary volunteers to take home photocopied material about three different countries, from which to highlight information for class next week. The material should focus on these areas: the political history of the country, what crops are raised, what resources are exported, the geography. Ask that the reports be brief and verbal. Encourage them to use pictures to supplement the material.

Session 4

Objective: To learn about the church in the Pacific islands and its history.

Resources:

Follow the Sun... to Western Samoa
Come to My Place
Map 'n' Facts

Introduction

Ask the children how they first heard about the church. They will most likely say through their families or through friends. Explain that, in one sense, that is also how people in the Pacific islands first learned and continue to learn today about the church and about Jesus. Some of the people who came to tell others about Jesus were called missionaries and most of our North American churches still have people who are missionaries somewhere in the world.

For Younger Children

Read to them, or have them read, the story paper material on Western Samoa and "Nafanua's Promise to Malietoa." To supplement it, refer to the material on the history of the church in *Come to My Place.*

Ask the children to think about what missionaries might do today. They could teach children to read or they could be doctors. What else could they do? They could also be teachers who would teach the Pacific island people skills, such as faster and easier ways to communicate, or ways to make their crops produce more. What things might you and I learn from Christians in the Pacific islands who would come to our country? Are there ways that we could grow as Christians?

If possible, have shells or seeds available for children to make necklaces. Or substitute various sizes of macaroni (especially "shell" macaroni).

If you prefer, ask the children to draw a picture of one thing they think missionaries might do today and put the pictures in the Big Book. Some children may wish to complete the activities suggested in "Keeping Your Trip Book" for this session.

For Older Children

Hear the reports from the children who volunteered in the previous session. Gather their information and place it in the learning center or a spot in the room that is accessible to all the children.

As a transition to talking about the history of the church, ask the children to think about how the countries reported on have changed in the past 100 or 200 years. What influences have encouraged change? Has all change been for the best? What might have been different?

Ask children to read the material on "People of Yesterday and Today" in *Come to My Place*. Different groups could read different sections and tell the rest of the class what they read.

In what ways has the world to which missionaries come changed? What do you think missionaries from the Pacific islands might say to us in North America today about our church and faith? Do you think we might also need missionaries? Why or why not?

What things might missionaries do in the Pacific islands today? (See material for younger children in this session.) If you were to be a missionary today, what could you give or bring that might be valuable? What would you want to learn from the people in the Pacific islands?

Follow-up Activity

List on newsprint the names of some countries that participate in the Pacific Conference of Churches. Refer to the material in *Map 'n' Facts* about the PCC. Ask children to think about what advantages there might be in a number of churches working together.

Think about a hymn that might be sung in the Pacific islands (such as the Doxology). Sing it together. Or use the song "Go Olraoni" from story paper 4.

Session 5

Objective: To celebrate things we have learned about the Pacific islands and, in a Pacific way, to celebrate with food.

Resources:

Follow the Sun... to Micronesia
Come to My Place
Map 'n' Facts
People of the Silver Sea

Introduction

If possible, plan for this to be an intergenerational event. Invite families to come together and share in the celebration. A family night supper might be a good time to do this.

For Younger Children

Read through the story "Where Am I?" Talk about the feelings of the child in the narrative. Has something like that ever happened to you? Complete the "Coconut Crossword Puzzle." When completed, talk about the answers, using this opportunity to gather together information the group has learned.

Work to complete the Big Book so that it can be shared during the celebration.

For Older Children

Use this time to prepare for the celebration by setting up displays of projects the group has completed. Some children may be going to give brief reports, perform a song or role play an episode from one of the stories for the total group, and they may need a brief rehearsal period.

Some children might like to prepare a fruit salad for the celebration. Use such fruits as mango, papaya and guava if you can find them, and pineapple, coconut, watermelon, oranges and bananas.

The Celebration

Children may wish to welcome their parents, siblings and other guests with flower necklaces. Like Pacific children, they could sit on mats on the floor during the celebration.

If **projects** the children have completed are on display, allow time for looking at these. Let the children act as guides, explaining what they have been doing.

Sing some of the **songs** learned during the sessions. Choose one or two to teach to the whole group. If songs have been printed in the Big Book, stand it up in front of the group so everyone can see the words. Pacific island people often use a guitar, small wooden drum or rhythm sticks to accompany their singing, or clap during the songs.

Read some entries from the Big Book. Pacific island children often learn to read in this way. Groups might read some of the lists of plants, animals and Pacific language words.

View the **filmstrip** as a group. Adults may find that they get a new perspective from the children's soundtrack. Talk about what you have learned.

Celebrate with food. Banana leaves are often spread on the floor like a tablecloth for an island feast. The children could sit around any big leaves spread on the floor. Refreshments could be as simple as several kinds of fruit or fruit salad and fruit juice, or you could plan a complete meal. Appropriate foods include avocados, yams (which resemble taro) and roast pig or some form of pork, chicken or fish.

At the conclusion of the celebration, invite participants to tell one thing they have learned about the Pacific islands and why it is important to them. Close with a brief worship period based on what you have learned during the study sessions.

5. Additional Resources

If you decide to order any materials directly from the Pacific or to contact any of the Pacific addresses given here, be sure to allow adequate mailing time. Allow a minimum of two weeks for your air mail inquiry to reach its destination, and another two weeks for the reply to reach you.

Books and Periodical Articles

The American Touch in Micronesia. David Nevin. New York: W.W. Norton, 1977. Describes U.S. influence in Micronesia and how North American values and cultural patterns are often superimposed over island cultures and values.

Beyond Pandemonium. Walter Lini. Wellington, N.Z.: Asia Pacific Books, 1980.

A Descriptive Atlas of the Pacific Islands. T.F. Kennedy. Wellington, N.Z.: Reed Education, 1974.

Development Is People: A Pacific View of Human Development. Suva, Fiji: Lotu Pasifika, 1976.

Faces of New Guinea. James Sinclair. Melbourne, Australia: Jacaranda Press, 1973.

The Island Churches of the South Pacific: Emergence in the Twentieth Century. Charles W. Forman. Maryknoll, N.Y.: Orbis Books, 1982. (Paper $17.50)

Mission, Church, and Sect in Oceania. James A. Boutilier, Daniel T. Hughes and Sharon W. Tiffany, eds. Ann Arbor: University of Michigan Press, 1978.

Moruroa Mon Amour: The French Nuclear Tests in the Pacific. B. and M. Danielsson. New York: Penguin, 1977.

New Hebrides: The Road to Independence. Chris Plant, ed. Suva, Fiji: Institute of Pacific Studies, University of the South Pacific, 1977.

The New South Pacific. R.G. Crocombe. Canberra, Australia: Australian National University Press, 1973. A survey of the contemporary Pacific world.

One Hundred Years in the Islands. Neville Threlfall. Papua New Guinea: Toksave na na Buk Depatmen, The United Church (New Guinea Islands Region), 1975.

Pacific Tourism: Contrasts in Values and Expectations. Cynthia Z. Biddlecomb. Suva, Fiji: Lotu Pasifika, 1981.

Song of the Pacific. RISK, vol. 12, no. 1. 1976. Published by the World Council of Churches and available from Room 772, 475 Riverside Drive, New York, NY 10115.

Women of Fiji. Sumitra Gokal. Suva, Fiji: Lotu Pasifika, 1978. Describes the significant role of women in the leadership of a developing and independent nation.

Women's Role in Fiji. Jyoti Amratlal, Eta Baro, Vanessa Griffen, Geet Bala Singh. Suva, Fiji: South Pacific Social Sciences Association (Box 5083), 1975.

"Micronesia: A Time of Hope Amidst Challenge," Mary Ann Smith. *Response*, July-August 1980.

"Trusteeship Council Welcomes 1981 Plebiscite Under UN Supervision on Future Status of Micronesia," *UN Chronicle*, vol. XVII, no. 7, August 1980.

For Teachers of Children

The following Friendship Press resources will help you plan studies on a wide variety of topics and belong in every teacher's library.

Clues to Creativity, vol. 1-3. M. Franklin and Maryann J. Dotts. $4.95 each. Detailed instructions on providing creative learning experiences for children.

Children's Festivals from Many Lands. Nina Millen, ed. $4.95.

Children's Games from Many Lands. Nina Millen, ed. $5.95.

Guidelines for Selecting Bias-Free Textbooks and Story Papers. Council on Interracial Books for Children, ed. $6.95.

The Whole World Singing. Edith Lovell Thomas. Paper $4.95, cloth $7.95.

Available from Intermedia

The following are available during this study year, in limited quantity, from David W. Briddell, Director, Intermedia, Room 670, 475 Riverside Drive, New York, NY 10115.

The Pacific Way — An Emerging Identity. Ron Crocombe. 1976. 56 pages, $2.50. An analysis of the Pacific way that probes beyond stereotypes and easy understandings.

Papua New Guinea, Land of Contrasts. David Holdsworth. 1980. 54 pages. Pictorial overview of the country, reflecting a nation in transition and undergoing rapid social change $5.00.

People of the Pacific Islands. David Holdsworth. Pictorial presentation of the peoples and cultures of the various regions of the Pacific islands $5.00.

Tok Pisin — The Easy Way. Frank Mihalic. 1982. 85 pages, $3.50. Simple guide to understanding the emerging indigenous language of Papua New Guinea.

Visuals of Papua New Guinea. 1981. $5.00. Packet of six black and white posters depicting the life and faith of Papua New Guinea Christians.

Addresses

The Pacific Conference of Churches and Lotu Pasifika Productions, P.O. Box 208, Suva, Fiji.

The Melanesian Institute (Sister Helen O'Brien, Editor), P.O. Box 571, Goroka, Papua New Guinea.

Office of Information, Papua New Guinea Government, Waigani, Papua New Guinea.

Office of Tourism, Papua New Guinea Government, P.O. Box 773, Port Moresby, Papua New Guinea.

United Nations Association of the U.S.A., Inc., National Office, 300 East 42nd Street, New York, NY 10017.

Miscellaneous

Change and Challenge in the South Pacific. Wallchart compiled and produced by CORSO National Office, 49 Courtenay Place, Wellington, New Zealand.

"Readings for Pacific Leaders on the Risks of Nuclear Technology," Pacific Conference of Churches, Suva, Fiji.

This song is used at the beginning and ending of the filmstrip *People of the Silver Sea.*

AT EASTER DAWN THERE'S A SILVER SEA

Words and music by John Garrett and Ta Makirere
Used by permission of Lotu Pasifika Productions

There was fu-ry that long week-end, Cai-a-phas was try-ing to be Cae-sar's friend. Yes, brother, don't pre-tend That we weren't there at all; We both saw him cru-ci-fied And on the cross he died. Yet at Easter Dawn there's a sil-ver sea Christ is ri-sen and we are free. He rose in a gar-den at break of day, He took our fears and all our sins a-way, Ma-ry heard; she heard him say, "I live, and love you all." So in the end the cru-ci-fied is liv-ing by our side. Yes, at Easter dawn there's a sil-ver sea Christ is ri-sen and we are free.

Piano accompaniment for this song may be ordered from Friendship Press Editorial Offices, Room 772, 475 Riverside Drive, New York, NY 10115 Send 25c and a stamped self-addressed envelope.